SONGWRITERS PLAYGROUND®

BARBARA L. JORDAN

First edition—1994. Printed in the United States of America.

Cover design by Blackmun Illustration/Design
Illustrations by Molly Brandenburg
Typesetting and Layout by David Willis

Library of Congress Cataloging in Publication Data

Jordan, Barbara, 1955-
       Songwriters playground / Barbara L. Jordan

       Includes bibliographical references.
       1. Music   I. Title.
                                                   93-72243

ISBN: 1-4392-0797-6

TABLE of CONTENTS

I'll play it first
and tell you what it is later.

—Miles Davis

INTRODUCTION

There are many books about the business and craft of songwriting, but as you will soon discover, this is not one of them.

Songwriters Playground is a book you *do*, not just read. You won't find in it any rules about writing better songs or tips about marketing them. What you *will* find is a series of provocative improvisatory exercises which will grab you by your creative lapels and propel you directly into songwriting. This book is designed to light your creative fires—and it will, if you let it!

As a professional songwriter and music supervisor for films and television, I spend a lot of time writing and listening to songs. Many songs are well-crafted—they follow the rules—but only a few stand out. The memorable ones have a magic and vitality which the others lack. The question is: Where does this special quality come from?

I can tell you with certainty that it doesn't come from craft alone. Several years ago, while suffering from extended writer's block, I worked hard at refining my craft. I read books, I took classes, I analyzed hit songs. And indeed, my craft improved—but at the expense of the magic. And writing songs was still a struggle.

I finally broke out of my songwriting ruts *not* by learning more rules but by intentionally setting them aside. Through a variety of techniques designed to set the right mood, stretch the creative muscles and get me writing quickly without any concern for brilliance, I suddenly found myself writing more and better songs faster than ever before. As a consequence, I not only started to enjoy songwriting again, but I began to have consistent success in the music business with my songs. Their newfound freshness and vitality were obviously contagious.

Since organizing the exercises into the Songwriters Playground workshops, I have watched many of my students experience the same transformation. By turning their whole consciousness into a kind of creative pinball machine with an infinite variety of outcomes, participants rediscover the thrill of experimentation and spontaneity in their writing. The workshops liberate songwriters from their struggle to reconcile the demands of the marketplace with their need for unrestricted self-expression. People are freed to "just do it." Chronic procrastinators start classes unable to begin writing, and by the end nothing can stop them!

I haven't yet found a way to bottle this elixir, but I am constantly asked for some kind of written guide to the Playground method. This book is the result. Like the workshops it has been a labor of much love. But because I am also a creative procrastinator, it is one which would not have been completed without the constant prodding and encouragement of my students. It is for them that I have made this attempt to anchor in book form the mercurial spirit of the workshops. I hope I have succeeded.

Welcome to the Playground!

Barbara Jordan
Los Angeles, CA

WHAT IS SONGWRITERS PLAYGROUND?

In the mind of the beginner, all things are possible,
But in the mind of the expert, only a few.
                    Zen Master Suzuki-Roshi
                    Zen Mind, Beginner's Mind

More than anything else, Songwriters Playground is about getting back into your Beginner's Mind *where all things are possible*, where judgment is intentionally suspended while the creative process is under way. It's about *creative spontaneous combustion* and the means for inducing it—*play.*

For songwriters—indeed, for all creative artists—play is very serious business! It is the primary pathway to the most fertile fields of the imagination. As children, we run up and down this path without thinking, but as we grow older and learn about all the things that *cannot be done*, the path becomes cluttered with obstacles. So gradually we use it less and less, until we have almost completely forgotten where it used to take us.

Songwriters Playground is a proven technique for bulldozing the creative pathways clear again. It gets you to *do* without thinking, to *write* without editing, to free-associate, experiment, take chances—all without fear or censorship. The Playground method is rooted in the unshakeable belief that you have more than enough good material inside you; you only have to find it and bring it out into the light. The more ideas you come up with, the more *gems* you will discover in the process. Quantity of output eventually produces quality—and truly vital songwriting—as long as you are first given the license to "lose your head."

Songwriters Playground is an open, improvisatory environment where you can loosen up and take some chances. Former participants in Playground workshops have found that although it may be difficult at first to shed writing inhibitions, by the end of the sessions their creative absorption is so intense that any blocks they might have been experiencing have dissolved. When you too have achieved this state of "controlled abandon," your songs will be infinitely more powerful and exciting than anything you have written previously.

How It Works

Why does this happen? *How* does this happen? It happens because you are free to write *whatever you want* as long as you write *as much as you can* in the time allotted for the Playground exercises. And the time allotted is impossibly short! That's the creative challenge which the Playground throws at you.

You begin every session by first shedding the persona you brought into the room. If you are self-conscious or overly cerebral to start with, the "Icebreaker Exercises" will loosen you up. You get a little "whack on the side of the head" to remind you not to take yourself or your writing too seriously.

In the second stage, the "Sense Exercises" bring your most vivid perceptions to the surface so that you can enliven your writing with them. Sounds, smells and images are used to trigger feelings and memories which might otherwise be unavailable to your conscious mind.

In the "Word Play Exercises" of the third stage, you toss around words, ideas and phrases, letting them fall where they may. The resulting serendipitous combinations of words, more commonly used in other ways, will startle you with their newfound poetry. By wandering through a verbal bazaar in this fashion, mixing and matching, all sorts of new ideas and images will occur to you.

In the Playground's fourth stage, the "Music Improv Exercises" push you out of your compositional ruts. They get you to break old musical habits and explore new chordal, rhythmic and melodic directions. Playground participants often remark, "Well, I never would have thought to play *that*—but it sounds great!"

In the "Now Write The Song" section, you pull order from the chaos. You are given 30 minutes to construct a song using as many of the previously generated lyrical and musical nuggets as possible. *This is where the alchemy occurs.* When faced with an imminent deadline, you are forced to settle for many of your first thoughts, which often turn out to be your best thoughts. This kind of pressure, in which highly focused, spontaneous writing occurs, results in songs that rarely fail to surprise and delight. "I've never written anything as good as this, or as quickly as this" is a common response. And that's exactly the response that Songwriters Playground is designed to elicit.

Songs That Soar

That's the five-stage program. It's deceptively simple, but it packs a real creative wallop. So much so, in fact, that a modest word of caution may be in order. Your first few experiences with Songwriters Playground may be somewhat unsettling. It is very common for Playground participants to lurch from serenity to anxiety, euphoria to wistfulness, relief to frustration, all in the same session. But don't let those feelings stop you—you're *supposed* to react that way. Someone once said "You can't sweep other people off their feet if you can't be swept off your own." Enjoy the roller coaster ride! And rest assured that if your songs capture even a fraction of your feelings, they will be living, breathing creations that living, breathing people will respond to.

Of course, not everything you write in the Playground will be something you want to keep. But you will be amazed at how many songs you *do* want to keep for later completion or revision. This is where the "Song Dialogue" (outlined in Part Three) can be of enormous help to you. Through this remarkable process, you engage in a candid conversation with the most knowledgeable and sympathetic critic you have ever encountered: your song itself. Your intuition will speak to you in the guise of your song, and you will learn precisely what it is your song may still need to get ready for the marketplace. Sound a little strange? Don't worry, it works! You'll see when you try it.

Chimps and Songwriters

By now, you can see that Songwriters Playground is really about awakening your amateur spirit—that is, the uncensored creative impulse from which all art springs. Craft alone is hollow. Songs with meaning, feeling and energy may get polished by the craftsman's hand, but they *originate* in the amateur heart.

Did you know that the word "amateur" is derived from a Latin word meaning "one who loves"? World-renowned zoologist Desmond Morris gave a group of chimpanzees canvas and paint, and watched as they became so absorbed in making paintings that they lost interest in the external world. They didn't care what anyone else thought; they were simply amateurs, in love with their creations. But when Morris subsequently rewarded the chimps for their paintings, guess what happened? Both the quality and the quantity of their work went down. They would do only enough painting to get the banana!

We have a lot in common with those chimpanzees. The focus on results and external rewards will almost certainly interrupt the creative state of mind referred to as "flow." How, then, can songwriters, hoping to bring their creative wares to the marketplace, silence the needy spirit crying "banana!" and write songs of beauty and power? By getting back to their amateur selves, their "beginners' minds" where all things are still possible.

The place to begin is right here, in the Songwriters Playground. Check your inhibitions at the gate, forget about what you think the world wants to hear, and start writing from the inside out. Songwriting can—and should—be fun!

Here we go!

P<small>ART</small> O<small>NE</small>

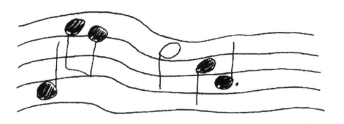

The Six-Week Program

R EAD T HIS F IRST

Part One leads you through a six-week program of exercises similar to an actual Songwriters Playground workshop. By following this program carefully, you will be able to master the basics and move on to the supplementary exercises in Part Two with more freedom and confidence.

WHAT YOU WILL NEED

Before starting a session, be sure you have on hand:

- ✔ a timer

- ✔ a hand-held tape recorder

- ✔ a pencil and notebook

- ✔ your musical instrument (if you play one)

PLAYGROUND FORMAT

Each Playground session will include the following four kinds of exercises to be performed in sequence:

- ◆ **ICEBREAKERS** — You're going to loosen up and get crazy here. Expect to feel really silly. That's the point.

- ◆ **SENSE EXERCISES** — Reconnects your physical senses with your writing. Brings you alive—don't fight it!

- ◆ **WORD PLAY** — Titles, lyric fragments, words and stories get tossed around. Don't think, just keep writing.

- ◆ **MUSIC IMPROVISATION** — Melody, chords and rhythm spill out in unexpected ways. Push the boundaries.

After completing the exercises, you will have 30 minutes to write as much of a song as you can using at least two of the elements generated by the exercises, such as title ideas, phrases, musical hooks, lyrical fragments, etc. You will then perform what you created.

Following each individual session, you will be given a **checklist** to make sure you have done the exercises correctly. *Don't skip it*—it will help make subsequent sessions even more productive.

Finally, you will have time before the next session to consider whether you want to develop further anything you created during the exercises. To help you with that determination, you may want to use the **Song Dialogue** process outlined in Part Three.

GETTING THE MOST OUT OF THE EXERCISES

☛ Read This Section Carefully

1. There are two ways to experience Songwriters Playground. You can do these exercises alone, or in a group with other songwriters. They are more fun in a group, but if you can't get a group together you can do them by yourself—provided you perform one additional step after each exercise: Tape record yourself reading aloud whatever you've written, any sounds you've made or music you've composed, and then play it back so you can hear yourself. *You mustn't ignore this step—it's important to hear the material coming back at you.*

If you are working with a group, make sure that after every *writing* exercise you take turns reading aloud what you have written to the group. Exercises involving movement, sounds or music are meant to be performed all together as a group or in sub-groups.

2. You'll notice time limits on each of the exercises. *Stick to them.* By limiting the time an exercise takes, the free flow of uncensored ideas is actually increased. Many of your best concepts, lyrics and musical ideas will spring from the accelerated stream of consciousness which results from this technique.

3. Whenever writing, keep the pencil moving across the page. Don't stop to think about what you should write next—you don't have the time anyway!

4. Don't omit any of the exercises, whether or not they seem to be either too elementary or too advanced for your current skill level. Give them a shot—very often, *any* attempt at these exercises will produce surprising results.

So, keeping these things in mind, go ahead and dive into your first set of exercises.

AND REMEMBER TO HAVE FUN!

WEEK ONE

PEOPLE WHO MAKE NO NOISE
ARE dANGEROUS.

—Jean delaFontaine

YOU ARE THE ALIEN
WHO JUST LANDED IN THIS SPACESHIP.

Talk in your native language and say anything
you like for 15 seconds.

Translate what you said into English.

The smell and taste of things
remain poised a long time, like souls...
waiting and hoping for their moment.

—Marcel Proust

RECALL A SMELL
THAT HAS SPECIAL MEANING FOR YOU...

someone's cologne...

your grandmother's
chicken soup...

a holiday tree, etc.

Write about it for 2 minutes.

All words are pegs
to hang ideas on.

—Harriet Beecher Stowe

VISUALIZE A BEACH SCENE.

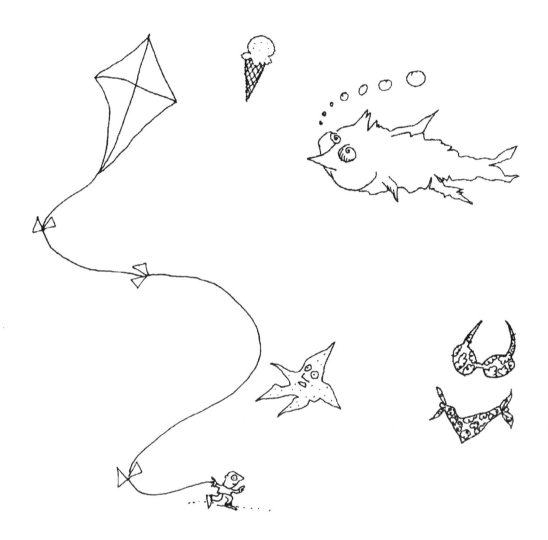

Take 1 minute to write down *things* you see there.
Then take 1 minute to write down *adjectives* describing things
at the beach (not necessarily relating to your first list.)
Now randomly combine words from both lists in any sequence.

Take 3 minutes total.

I love to write songs over lyrics.
I start to read the lyrics like a poem,
and try to find the movement of the words.

—Ivan Lins

RANDOMLY SELECT ONE SHORT SENTENCE
FROM *ANY* TEXT.

Read it over and over, until you feel it take on a rhythm...
and the rise and fall of a melody line.
Now sing *just* the melody.

Take 30 seconds total.

NOW...**WRITE THE SONG!**

Pick **at least two** elements from the previous exercises — such as title ideas, phrases, musical hooks, lyrical fragments, etc. — which seem like enough to get a song started. For example, one or two words may already be a title; a word or phrase may become a line of lyric; an unusual sound you made could be incorporated into your music track; or a melody fragment could be utilized by the voice, bass or other instrument.

Take **30 minutes** (no more than that) to write as much of a song as you can. (If you are working in a group, break into collaborative sub-groups of two to four people per group.) Don't worry about producing a masterpiece — just produce as much as you can in the allotted time with the materials at hand. You may have some great material to work with; or you may think it's all junk! Either way, pick at least two things to start with and get going.

When the time is up, perform and record whatever you created.

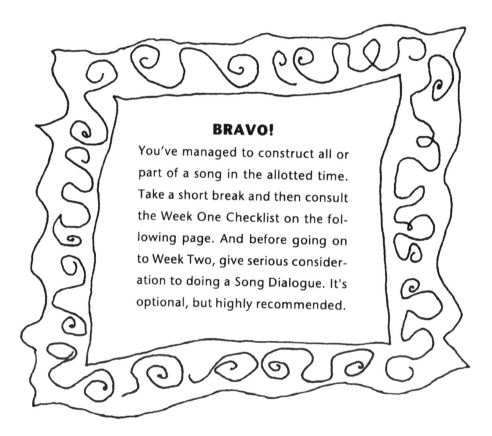

BRAVO!

You've managed to construct all or part of a song in the allotted time. Take a short break and then consult the Week One Checklist on the following page. And before going on to Week Two, give serious consideration to doing a Song Dialogue. It's optional, but highly recommended.

WEEK ONE CHECKLIST

1. In the **Spaceship** exercise:
   a) Did you experiment with a new vocal sound?
   b) Did you feel silly and irrational?
   c) If in a group, did several of you aliens speak to each other?
   d) If alone, did you tape yourself talking and then listen back to it?

2. In the **Smell** exercise:
   a) Did you keep your pencil moving, not stopping to analyze your writing?
   b) When you read your writing aloud, did you just read it back without making editorial comments?
   c) If alone, did you tape record yourself reading what you had written and then listen back to it?

3. In the **Beach Scene** exercise:
   a) In the third list, did you put words together randomly in no special order?
   b) Did you discover some interesting combinations?
   c) If in a group, did you read back what you had written to the other participants?
   d) If alone, did you read what you had written into a tape recorder and then play it back?

4. In the **Select-A-Sentence** exercise:
   a) As you read your text, did you hear a melody in your vocal inflection?
   b) Did you then sing the melody by itself with no words?
   c) Was the sentence you selected short enough so that the melody was easy to remember?
   d) If in a group, did you take turns singing your melodies?
   e) If alone, did you tape record yourself and then play it back?

5. In the **Now Write The Song** wrap-up:
   a) Did you quickly grab at least 2 "ingredients" from the previous exercises to start with?
   b) Did you stop writing when the 30 minutes were up?

   ――――――――――――――――

You may be surprised — and pleased — by the song you produced in this session. If so, you might be tempted to finish or "fix" it afterwards. But before you subject it to your Inner Critic (who only hangs out *outside* of the Playground), please turn to the section on **Song Dialogue** beginning on page 103. Let it tell you what the song really needs.

W EEK T WO

If anything is worth doing at all,
it's worth doing badly.

—Gustav Holst

CRUSH THREE PIECES OF PAPER INTO THE SHAPE OF BALLS.

Juggle them as well as you can.

Take 1 minute.

The body is the soul.

—Theodore Roethke

LIST ANY HEIGHTENED PHYSICAL SENSATIONS
YOU CAN RECALL SUCH AS...

the rush of skiing,

the pain of
a toothache, etc.

Take 1 minute.

It's just something a little out of the ordinary
in terms of a mental stimulus...like a trigger.

—Eric Clapton

TAKE 15 SECONDS TO LOOK AROUND THE ROOM
AND CHOOSE THREE OBJECTS.

Write a story incorporating these three objects.

Take 2 minutes.

The fact is, there are no rules,
and there never were any rules,
and there will never be any rules
of musical composition except rules of thumb;
and thumbs vary in length, like ears.

—George Bernard Shaw

STATE ONE *MUSICAL* RULE OF SONGWRITING
YOU WOULD NEVER CONSIDER BREAKING.

Now... BREAK that rule!

Take 5 minutes.

NOW...**WRITE THE SONG!**

Pick **at least two** elements from the previous exercises — such as title ideas, phrases, musical hooks, lyrical fragments, etc. — which seem like enough to get a song started. For example, one or two words may already be a title; a word or phrase may become a line of lyric; an unusual sound you made could be incorporated into your music track; or a melody fragment could be utilized by the voice, bass or other instrument.

Take **30 minutes** (no more than that) to write as much of a song as you can. (If you are working in a group, break into collaborative sub-groups of two to four people per group.) Don't worry about producing a masterpiece — just produce as much as you can in the allotted time with the materials at hand. You may have some great material to work with; or you may think it's all junk! Either way, pick at least two things to start with and get going.

When the time is up, perform and record whatever you created.

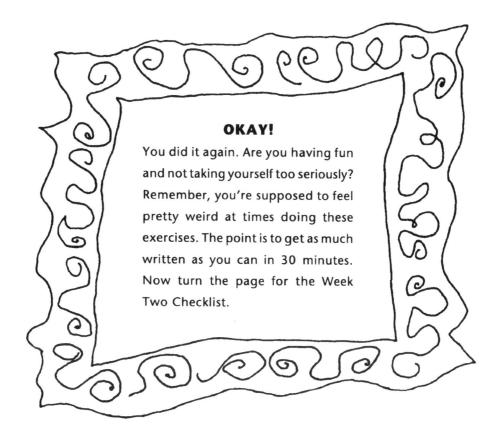

OKAY!

You did it again. Are you having fun and not taking yourself too seriously? Remember, you're supposed to feel pretty weird at times doing these exercises. The point is to get as much written as you can in 30 minutes. Now turn the page for the Week Two Checklist.

WEEK TWO CHECKLIST

1. In the **Juggling** exercise:
   a) Did you have fun, even if you couldn't juggle properly?
   b) Did you like at least trying to do something new?
   c) Did you move around? If in a group, did you bump into other people? Did you feel a little out of breath?

2. In the **Physical Sensation** exercise:
   a) Did you try to recall as many physical sensations as possible?
   b) Did it make you feel something, either physical or emotional, to write down these things?
   c) Did you write in short, concrete phrases and not worry about complete grammatical sentences?
   d) Did you read exactly what you wrote aloud, not commenting on it?

3. In the **Three Object** exercise:
   a) Did you find a way to put all three objects into a story?
   b) Did you keep your pencil going, even if none of it seemed to be making sense to your rational mind?
   c) Did you stop when the timer rang?
   d) After writing, did you read your story out loud without trying to clean up grammatical errors and "stupid stuff?"

4. In the **Musical Rule** exercise:
   a) Did you consciously try to write a chord progression or melody you might previously have thought to be wrong or prohibited?
   b) Did you find a way to break the rule and still create music?
   c) Did you perform the results for your group or your tape recorder and then listen back?

5. In the **Now Write The Song** wrap-up:
   a) Did you feel hurried and often have to settle for your first thoughts?
   b) Did you perform and record whatever song or song fragment you came up with?

_____

How about doing a **Song Dialogue**? Turn to page 103 for instructions.

WEEK THREE

You will do foolish things,
but do them with enthusiasm.

—Colette

CHOOSE TO BECOME:

either
a liquid,

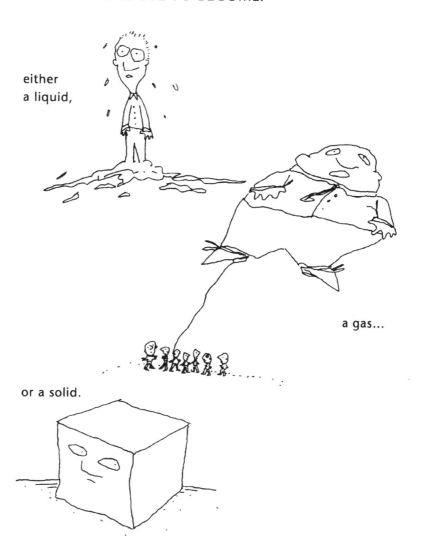

a gas...

or a solid.

Use your whole body to become that property and
move around the room as much as you like.

Stay in character for 1 minute.

A juq of winE
A loaf of bread
And thou

—The Rubaiyat of Omar Khayyam

THINK OF A MEMORABLE MEAL YOU'VE EATEN
AT SOME TIME IN YOUR LIFE.

In as much detail as possible, write about the experience.

Take 2 minutes.

"Rene and Georgette Magritte
With Their Dog After the War"
comes from a photograph ...
of Rene and Georgette with their dog.

—Paul Simon

GET A PHOTO FROM SOMEONE ELSE'S PHOTO ALBUM
OR RANDOMLY SELECT A PHOTO FROM A BOOK.

Look at the photo and write as many short phrases
as come to mind.

Take 1 minute.

A lot of the time I start off with a feel, just a few chords...
allowing the unexpected to happen.

—Lindsey Buckingham

WRITE A CHORD PROGRESSION USING THREE CHORDS.

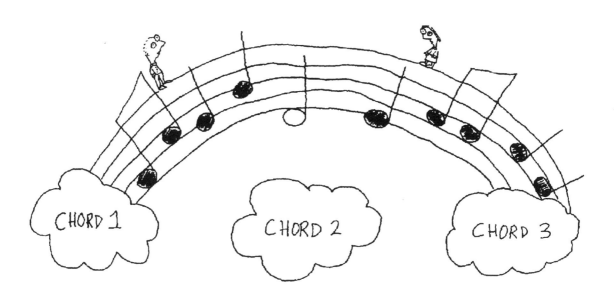

Write a melody over those three chords.
Now add onto or vary this musical fragment.

Take 5 minutes.

NOW...**WRITE THE SONG!**

Pick **at least two** elements from the previous exercises — such as title ideas, phrases, musical hooks, lyrical fragments, etc. — which seem like enough to get a song started. For example, one or two words may already be a title; a word or phrase may become a line of lyric; an unusual sound you made could be incorporated into your music track; or a melody fragment could be utilized by the voice, bass or other instrument.

Take **30 minutes** (no more than that) to write as much of a song as you can. (If you are working in a group, break into collaborative sub-groups of two to four people per group.) Don't worry about producing a masterpiece — just produce as much as you can in the allotted time with the materials at hand. You may have some great material to work with; or you may think it's all junk! Either way, pick at least two things to start with and get going.

When the time is up, perform and record whatever you created.

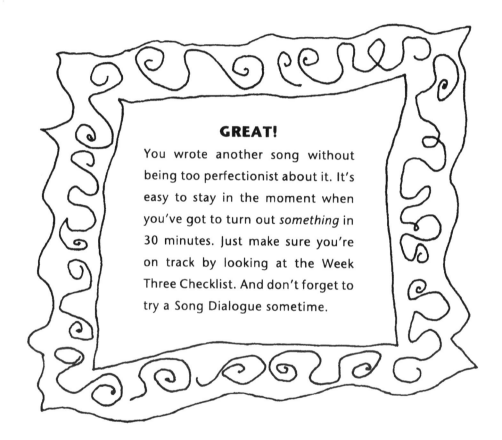

GREAT!

You wrote another song without being too perfectionist about it. It's easy to stay in the moment when you've got to turn out *something* in 30 minutes. Just make sure you're on track by looking at the Week Three Checklist. And don't forget to try a Song Dialogue sometime.

WEEK THREE CHECKLIST

1. In the **Liquid-Gas-Solid** exercise:
   a) Did you move around and overcome your inhibitions about acting silly?
   b) Did you feel like you got out of your own skin for a little while?
   c) Was it a relief to be something other than yourself?

2. In the **Memorable Meal** exercise:
   a) If you didn't remember a specific meal, did you make one up?
   b) Did you not worry whether you filled the whole page or wrote only one word?
   c) Did you recall the place, the time and the people who might have been there? Also, the colors, flavors and aromas of the food?
   d) If something disturbing came up, did you just continue with your writing?

3. In the **Photo** exercise:
   a) Did the photo you selected seem ordinary at first?
   b) Did you try to come up with as many short, caption-like phrases as possible and not worry about writing complete sentences?
   c) Did you simply try to write something descriptive rather than "interesting?"

4. In the **Chord/Melody** exercise:
   a) If you are not a musician, did you find a way to make some kind of melody?
   b) Did you add a link to your initial musical fragment?
   c) Did you tell yourself that you only had to try it — not necessarily love the results?

5. In the **Now Write The Song** wrap-up:
   a) Did you manage to write as much as you could in 30 minutes, without reprimanding yourself about the developing song's apparent flaws?
   b) Did the speed that you were forced to work at help you to stay intensely focused on the task at hand?

How about doing a **Song Dialogue**? Turn to page 103 for instructions.

WEEK FOUR

If your heart catches in your throat,
ask a bird how she sings.

—Cooper Edens

SELECT AN ANIMAL, PLANT, FRUIT, OR INSECT YOU'D LIKE TO BE.

In the first person, write about what it's like to be you.

Take 2 minutes.

Music is perpetual,
and only hearing is intermittent.

—Henry David Thoreau

LIST THE SOUNDS YOU'VE HEARD TODAY
FROM THE TIME YOU WOKE UP TO THIS MOMENT.

Take 1 minute.

The only Maybellene I ever knew
was a cow.

—Chuck Berry

GET A PHONE BOOK AND OPEN TO A RANDOM PAGE.

Find a name or street address that appeals to you and then
write about the person or street.

Take 2 minutes.

Music hath charms to soothe a savage breast,
to soften rocks, or bend a knotted oak.

—William Congreve

WRITE SOME MUSIC
YOU IMAGINE MIGHT HEAL SOMEONE WHO IS ILL.

Take 5 minutes.

NOW...**WRITE THE SONG!**

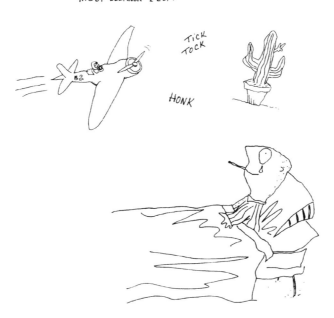

Pick **at least two** elements from the previous exercises — such as title ideas, phrases, musical hooks, lyrical fragments, etc. — which seem like enough to get a song started. For example, one or two words may already be a title; a word or phrase may become a line of lyric; an unusual sound you made could be incorporated into your music track; or a melody fragment could be utilized by the voice, bass or other instrument.

Take **30 minutes** (no more than that) to write as much of a song as you can. (If you are working in a group, break into collaborative sub-groups of two to four people per group.) Don't worry about producing a masterpiece — just produce as much as you can in the allotted time with the materials at hand. You may have some great material to work with; or you may think it's all junk! Either way, pick at least two things to start with and get going.

When the time is up, perform and record whatever you created.

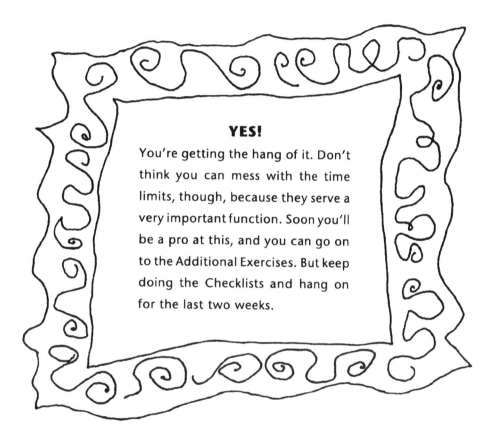

YES!

You're getting the hang of it. Don't think you can mess with the time limits, though, because they serve a very important function. Soon you'll be a pro at this, and you can go on to the Additional Exercises. But keep doing the Checklists and hang on for the last two weeks.

WEEK FOUR CHECKLIST

1. In the **Animal-Plant-Fruit** exercise:

   a) Did you remember to write *as* the object, not *about* the object?

   b) Did you experience the world from its perspective and identify with it?

   c) Did you describe what you saw and felt in concrete terms?

2. In the **Sounds** exercise:

   a) Did you become more aware of the background sounds you usually ignore?

   b) Did you try closing your eyes to intensify your hearing?

   c) Did you keep your descriptions on a literal plane and not use fancy language just to show off?

3. In the **Phonebook** exercise:

   a) Did you make your choice randomly from the first double page you opened to?

   b) Did you have fun inventing a story about the name or address you selected?

   c) Did you read aloud what you wrote?

4. In the **Healing Music** exercise:

   a) Was your melody or music track soothing or therapeutic in some way?

   b) Did you let yourself write from the heart and not your mind?

   c) If alone, did you record what you wrote and play it back?

5. In the **Now Write The Song** wrap-up:

   a) Did you feel the freedom to play around a little, writing as much or as little as the limited time allowed?

   b) Was the inner critic of secondary importance to the clock?

How about doing a **Song Dialogue**? Turn to page 103 for instructions.

WEEK FIVE

You have to have no inhibitions...
because if you're playing it safe all the time,
then nothing really new happens.

—Phil Collins

CHOOSE *ONE* OF THE FOLLOWING:

an insect

a jungle
animal

a reptile
or bird

or a barnyard animal.

Recreate the sound it makes.
(Don't forget to record it.)

Take 30 seconds.

"STRAWBERRY FIELDS FOREVER"

—The Beatles

LOOK AROUND THE ROOM AND PICK A PRIMARY COLOR.

Color: _Red_

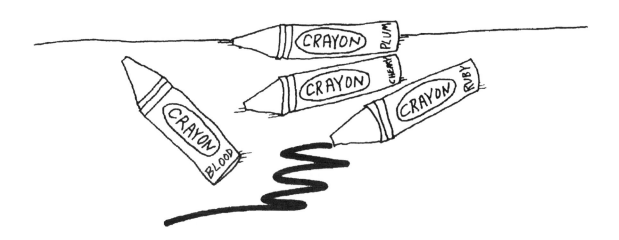

Notice objects that are varying shades of that color.
List the different shades you see.

Take 2 minutes.

Ah, good taste!
What a dreadful thing.
Taste is the enemy of creativeness.

—Pablo Picasso

WRITE THE WORST LYRIC YOU POSSIBLY CAN.

Be as tasteless, rude, angry or ridiculous as you want to be.

Write for 3 minutes.

Music itself is an amorphous, abstract,
intuitive, body-centered item...
but the road to that is based on a certain kind of understood order.

—Jennifer Warnes

CREATE A MUSICAL MOTIF
(BASS LINE, MELODY OR CHORD PROGRESSION)
FROM THE CONSONANTS AND VOWELS IN YOUR OWN NAME.

Construct a music track from this motif.

Take 5 minutes.

NOW...**WRITE THE SONG!**

Pick **at least two** elements from the previous exercises — such as title ideas, phrases, musical hooks, lyrical fragments, etc. — which seem like enough to get a song started. For example, one or two words may already be a title; a word or phrase may become a line of lyric; an unusual sound you made could be incorporated into your music track; or a melody fragment could be utilized by the voice, bass or other instrument.

Take **30 minutes** (no more than that) to write as much of a song as you can. (If you are working in a group, break into collaborative sub-groups of two to four people per group.) Don't worry about producing a masterpiece — just produce as much as you can in the allotted time with the materials at hand. You may have some great material to work with; or you may think it's all junk! Either way, pick at least two things to start with and get going.

When the time is up, perform and record whatever you created.

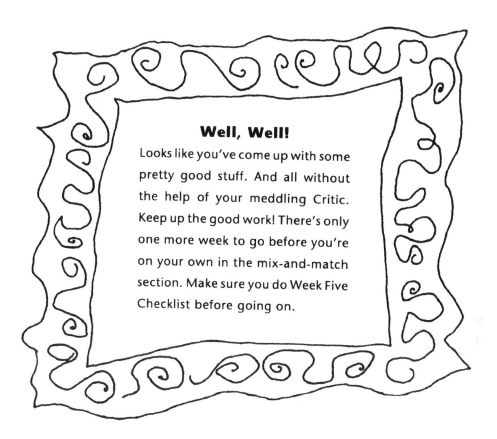

Well, Well!

Looks like you've come up with some pretty good stuff. And all without the help of your meddling Critic. Keep up the good work! There's only one more week to go before you're on your own in the mix-and-match section. Make sure you do Week Five Checklist before going on.

WEEK FIVE CHECKLIST

1. In the **Insect-Animal** exercise:
   a) Did you get a kick out of making this kind of sound?
   b) Did you feel more loosened up afterwards — or just ridiculous?
   c) If in a group, did you all make sounds at the same time?
   d) If alone, did you tape yourself and then listen back?

2. In the **Color Shades** exercise:
   a) Did you select a basic color first, and then look for various shades of that color around you?
   b) Did you come up with a good mix of nouns, adjectives and adverbs to describe the colors?
   c) Did you read the words aloud?

3. In the **Worst Lyric** exercise:
   a) Were you able to write without preconceptions about what a lyric ought to be?
   b) Did you let yourself go without any concern for what others might think?
   c) Did you say what you wanted to say without concern for rhyme or meter?

4. In the **Notes-In-Your-Name** exercise:
   a) If your name had no notes, did you use someone else's name or make one up?
   b) Did a non-musical source lead to a valid musical idea?
   c) Did you consider all the possibilities: melody, bass line, chord progression or motif?

5. In the **Now Write The Song** wrap-up:
   a) Did you remind yourself that you had to keep writing just so you'd have a product of *some* sort at the session's end?
   b) Did you make your best effort to pull together a few nuggets from the former exercises as the basis for your new composition?

How about doing a **Song Dialogue**? Turn to page 103 for instructions.

WEEK SIX

Imagination
is more important than knowledge.

—Albert Einstein

PUT ON AN ARTICLE OF CLOTHING OR ACCESSORY
THAT ISN'T YOURS.

Walk around in it for one minute and notice how it feels.
Write about a person who might own this object.

Take 3 minutes.

First we see
the hills in the painting.
Then we see
the painting in the hills.

—Li Li Wang

PICK AN OBJECT IN THE ROOM AND LOOK AT IT.

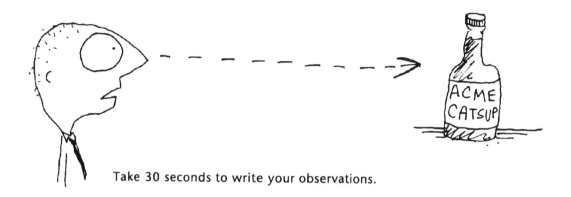

Take 30 seconds to write your observations.

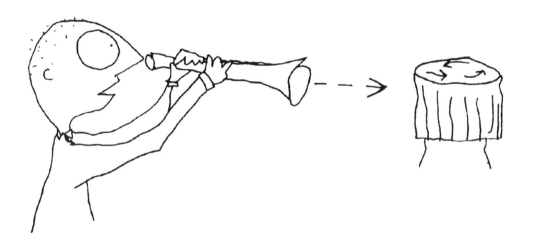

Now, roll up a piece of paper in the shape of a telescope
and focus it on the same object. Write
about what you see now.

Take 1 minute.

But I could have told you, Vincent,
This world was never meant
for one as beautiful as you.
Starry, starry night...

—Don McLean

WRITE A TRIBUTE TO SOMEONE:
A LITERARY CHARACTER, FILM STAR, OR ANYONE YOU ADMIRE.

Sigmund Freud

Lucille Ball

Honest Abe

Take 1 minute.

INTEREST IN THE CHANGING SEASONS
is a much happier state of mind
than being hopelessly in love with spring.

—George Santayana

THINK OF A PIECE OF MUSIC
FROM ANOTHER ERA OR CULTURE.

Using some element of that music as a starting point,
create a verse or chorus in a contemporary musical style of your choice.

Take 5 minutes.

NOW...**WRITE THE SONG!**

Pick **at least two** elements from the previous exercises — such as title ideas, phrases, musical hooks, lyrical fragments, etc. — which seem like enough to get a song started. For example, one or two words may already be a title; a word or phrase may become a line of lyric; an unusual sound you made could be incorporated into your music track; or a melody fragment could be utilized by the voice, bass or other instrument.

Take **30 minutes** (no more than that) to write as much of a song as you can. (If you are working in a group, break into collaborative sub-groups of two to four people per group.) Don't worry about producing a masterpiece — just produce as much as you can in the allotted time with the materials at hand. You may have some great material to work with; or you may think it's all junk! Either way, pick at least two things to start with and get going.

When the time is up, perform and record whatever you created.

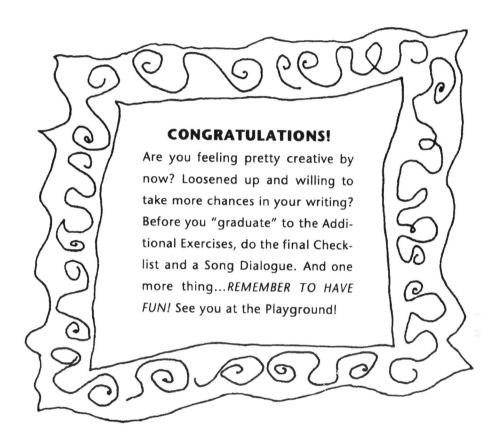

CONGRATULATIONS!
Are you feeling pretty creative by now? Loosened up and willing to take more chances in your writing? Before you "graduate" to the Additional Exercises, do the final Checklist and a Song Dialogue. And one more thing...*REMEMBER TO HAVE FUN!* See you at the Playground!

WEEK SIX CHECKLIST

1. In the **Dress-Up** exercise:
   a) Did you feel a little strange wearing something belonging to someone else?
   b) While wearing the item, did you identify more closely with its owner?
   c) Did you feel like you were moving through someone else's spiritual landscape?

2. In the **Telescope** exercise:
   a) Did the object you looked at change in any way when you telescoped it?
   b) Did it seem to take on a new intensity?
   c) Did the framing effect of the telescope produce a new visual universe?
   d) Did you write without concern for whether your writing sounded awkward in any way?

3. In the **Tribute** exercise:
   a) Did you write as if you were the person giving the tribute?
   b) Did you address the honoree directly, as though he or she might be listening to you?
   c) Did you say what *you* wanted to say to that person and not just what the rest of the world might say?

4. In the **Historic/Foreign Music** exercise:
   a) Did you use a foreign melodic scale, an exotic instrument, an historical form, etc. as the catalyst for your composition?
   b) Did your composition have a sense of timelessness?
   c) Did you feel like you had never written anything quite like this before? Did it seem fresh to you?

5. In the **Now Write The Song** wrap-up:
   a) Did you feel free of the burden to create a 30-minute masterpiece?
   b) Did hurrying make you any more willing than usual to silence the Inner Critic's harangues?

How about doing a **Song Dialogue**? Turn to page 103 for instructions.

PART TWO

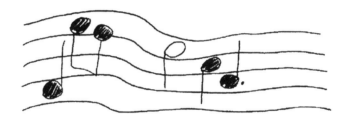

Additional Exercises

GROUP FORMAT

The following steps will guide your group through a complete Songwriters Playground session using the Additional Exercises. NOTE: WHENEVER WRITING IS INVOLVED, PARTICIPANTS SHOULD READ THEIR WRITINGS ALOUD TO THE GROUP.

1. Choose one **Icebreaker** exercise for the entire group to perform.

2. Choose one **Sense** exercise for the entire group to perform.

3. Choose one **Word Play** exercise for the entire group to perform.

4. Choose one **Music Improv** exercise and perform it. Break into sub-groups of two to four people if necessary. Tape record all musical ideas.

5. Break into collaborative groups of two to four participants per group. Allow yourselves no more than 30 minutes to write as much of a song as you can, using at least two of the elements generated from the previous exercises, such as title ideas, phrases, musical hooks, lyrical fragments, etc. When the time is up, perform whatever you created for the entire group. Don't forget to record your performance.

If the song warrants completion, finish it outside of the Playground time. (See the section on Song Dialogue, beginning on page 103.)

SOLO FORMAT

The following steps will guide you through a complete Songwriters Playground session using the Additional Exercises. NOTE: WHEN-EVER READING ALOUD, WRITING, OR MAKING SOUNDS, RECORD YOURSELF ON TAPE AND THEN LISTEN TO IT.

1. Choose one **Icebreaker** exercise and perform it.

2. Choose one **Sense** exercise and perform it.

3. Choose one **Word Play** exercise and perform it.

4. Choose one **Music Improv** exercise and perform it. Tape record all musical ideas.

5. Allow yourself no more than 30 minutes to write as much of a song as you can, using at least two of the elements generated from the previous exercises, such as title ideas, phrases, musical hooks, lyrical fragments, etc. When the time is up, perform and record whatever you created.

If the song warrants completion, finish it outside of the Playground time. (See the section on Song Dialogue, beginning on page 103.)

ICEBREAKER EXERCISES

Note: All Icebreaker Exercises are meant to be spoken or acted out, not written.

1. Make up a sentence that begins a story. Add to the story, a sentence at a time. Be as daffy or as illogical as you like. Take no more than 2 minutes.

2. Look around the room and select one object. While holding it and examining it more closely, free associate on all the possible uses for this object, no matter how bizarre or outlandish. Take 1 minute.

3. Using either melody or rhythm as your language, have a dialogue with yourself or another person. Take 30 seconds.

4. Make up a sentence such as "Last night I came out of the Palladium and my car was stolen." Now "translate" it into a foreign language you don't understand. Indicate what the language is. Take 30 seconds total.

5. Using five or fewer of any group of objects from your desk, pockets or purse, create a "picture" of something. Tell us what it is. Take 1 minute.

6. Invent an imaginary word. Say it out loud, and then define it in a sentence or two. Take 30 seconds.

7. Play some uptempo symphonic music, either from the radio or on tape. Pretend you are controlling the music by keeping the beat going with five different parts of your body (in sequence). Take 1 minute.

8. Invent a name for a new frozen dessert. Describe the ingredients. Take 1 minute.

9. Ask a "why" question and then invent an off-the-wall answer. For example — Question: "Why do volcanos spew out lava?" Answer: "Because they don't have enough pepto-bismol to keep from throwing up when the earth quakes." Take 30 seconds.

(To be done in a group.)

10. The first person begins a rhythm pattern using hands or feet, and keeps it steady. One at a time, the rest of the group layers additional patterns over it. Take 2 minutes.

SENSE EXERCISES

Note: All Sense Exercises are to be written and then read aloud.

1.   What emotions or physical sensations are you experiencing right now? Describe them purely objectively, without analysis or explanations of any sort. Take 1 minute.

2.   Look around the room and choose one object. For 1 minute, write down a few characteristics or properties of that object. Then take a look around again, and notice what other objects share some of those properties. List those objects and their similarities. Take 2 minutes.

3.   Think of someone you have never seen or met, but have talked to on the telephone. Write for 2 minutes about what you imagine this person to look like and be like based on his or her name and voice.

4.   Think of someone you don't know very well. Imagine in detail what they might be daydreaming about right now. Write about it for 2 minutes.

5.   Select any color crayon you like and draw and/or write whatever you want. Do at least half of it with your eyes closed. Don't think about it and don't make any corrections. Take 3 minutes.

6.   Turn on the radio and spin the dial to the first station that has music. Listen to it for 30 seconds. How does the music make you feel? Write about it for 15 seconds.

7. Imagine that you can become the opposite sex for one day out of every month. Describe what you would do on that day. Take 2 minutes.

8. Recall as many experiences as you can of deep spiritual feelings, either painful or joyous. In 2 minutes, identify them.

9. Close your eyes while one person walks around the group three times. Using your other senses, tune in to this person's "presence." Now open your eyes and write about it for 30 seconds. If alone, close your eyes and tune in to your own presence as you stand up and move around.

10. If you could fly, where would you be flying right now? Describe your flight. Take 2 minutes.

WORD PLAY EXERCISES

Note: All Word Play Exercises are to be written and then read aloud.

1. Cut out snippets of graphics or text from a magazine; arrange or paste them onto a white paper 8$\frac{1}{2}$ X 11 inches or larger. When you are finished, write a caption for it. Read it out loud and display your artwork. Take up to 10 minutes.

2. In the middle of a piece of paper, write in one short sentence something you need to express to someone in your life but are reluctant to say. Take 30 seconds. Then crumple it into a ball and toss it to the center of the table. Now open it up, read it and respond to it as if it were addressed to *you*. Write your response in 2 minutes.

3. Turn on the tv set and watch a movie for 5 minutes, listening for good titles, words or phrases to write down. If there are commercials, pay attention to them as well.

4. Find an article in a newspaper or magazine that intrigues you. Using the story as a springboard, write something in the first person that relates in some way to that story. Take 5 minutes.

5. Light a candle and darken the room. Have someone talk for 2 minutes about something embarrassing that once happened to them. After you have heard the story, turn the lights back on and take 1 minute to write down any memorable words or phrases you recall. If alone, talk into a tape recorder and then listen back.

6. Ask someone to talk for 3 minutes about what is happening romantically in his or her life right now. As you are listening, write down any words or phrases that sound like possible titles. If you are alone, first talk into a tape recorder; then as you listen to the playback, write down words or phrases that sound like titles.

7. Open to a page of text in a magazine. Circle any words you find that could be used as or in a title. Take 2 minutes to list as many of these words as you find.

8. What short phrase — seven words or less — would you have an airplane skywrite across the sky if you were sure the person you were addressing it to, dead or alive, would see it? Take 1 minute.

9. Dig out an old lyric of yours. Cut out each word, put them in a paper bag and shake them up. One by one, pull out the words and place them in an order that can't be rearranged. The new lyric doesn't have to make any sense. Take 5 minutes.

10. Recall any dream that is particularly memorable or that you have dreamed repeatedly. Write it down just as you remember it without analyzing it. Afterwards, circle any title ideas or interesting phrases. Take 2 minutes.

Music Improv Exercises

Note: All Music Improvisation Exercises are meant to be recorded while doing them (so you don't forget).

1.   Take 5 minutes to write a chorus (melody or melody and chords). Perform it. Then take 5 minutes to cut out half of the notes. Perform the new version.

2.   Using as accompaniment a musical instrument you've never learned to play, or any non-musical instrument hanging around, play anything as you sing a melody with words over the accompaniment. Take 3 minutes.

3.   Get out a music book with a collection of hit songs. Find one you don't recognize, and from one verse and chorus write down the chords it uses. Now write or sing your *own* melody to that chord progresssion. Take 10 minutes.

4.   Invent a new dance and write the chorus, words and melody for the song that represents it—e.g., "Walk Like An Egyptian" or "Walk the Dinosaur." Take 5 minutes.

5.   Write or sing a line of melody into your tape recorder. Now forget about the melody and write a chord progression with no connection to the melody. Play the two together and listen. Take 2 minutes.

6.   Using your body, or any available object, play a rhythmic pattern. Freely sing melodies over that pattern for 5 minutes.

7. Pretend you are a conductor in front of a full symphony orchestra. As you wave your arms and move your body for emphasis, sing a grand and emotional melody — compose it on the spot for the orchestra to play. Take 30 seconds.

8. Think of a song you like (not your own). Clap to its rhythm and sing its chorus. Now forget the song, but while continuing to clap its rhythm, write as much of a new song as you can over that beat, words and melody included. Take 10 minutes.

9. Play a sequence of 4 chords you like. Now scramble the chords into a new sequence you don't like. Improvise melodies over this new chord progression until it begins to sound pleasing to you. Take 5 minutes.

10. Look at your bookcase and find a book title you like. Set it to music two very different ways, both melodically and rhythmically. Take 1 minute.

PART THREE

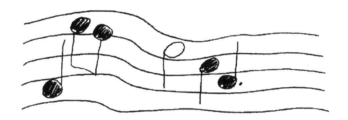

Song Dialogue

In each of us there is a king.
Speak to him and he will come forth.

—A Norse Saying

Song Dialogue

A partially written song may or may not warrant completion. The only way to find out is to ask it. Simply put, you will become a playwright, writing a mini-play in which the characters are you and your song. You'll have a dialogue on paper.

Begin by stating the reason you wish to have this song dialogue. Then move on to the actual conversation. It's important not to think too much — make sure you keep the pencil moving. Discuss mutual concerns. Just shoot the breeze.

Continue until it feels right to stop and then read aloud what you've written. You'll be amazed at what you learn, and you might even find the precise puzzle piece to your unfinished song.

If you are used to looking outside yourself for critique, the song dialogue will help you turn the process around. Give it a chance. As you get more comfortable with this technique, you'll find that your inner voice has much to tell you.

Here's a sample dialogue:

Statement: I'd like to know if I ought to dig out my old song "Pale Rider" (PR) and re-demo it so I can pitch it to the industry.

Me: Hi Song!

PR: *Howdy Partner. What's up?*

Me: I liked you a lot when I wrote you, and every time I happen to stumble upon you in my drawer, I listen to you and get excited again.

PR: *I'm pretty sexy, aren't I?*

Me: Yeh, as a matter of fact. But I always felt you were incomplete. Something about the chorus...

PR: *Are you sure you didn't get that idea from Pete, who listened to me and made some comments to that effect?*

Me: You've got a point. So, was he right?

PR: *You tell me, Babs.*

Me: Well, I don't get bored listening to you...

PR: *That's a good sign.*

Me: But... I suspect the world wouldn't respond the same way. After all, you're just a song inspired by a little Clint Eastwood movie.

PR: *Hey, that movie was a hit. A lot of people know about Pale Rider.*

Me: We're getting off the track. I need to know if I should demo you.

PR: *You already did.*

Me: Yeh, but not a fancy demo. You need some special packaging.

PR: *Like what kind of packaging?*

Me: Like a sexy R & B singer and a better drum track.

PR: *But you're getting off the track now...what about the song that I am? Am I developed enough yet to be demoed?*

Me: NO! The chorus needs work.

PR: *I'm glad you can say that. You see, I don't cycle very well in the chorus. It is boring to me, so I think you should come up with some alternative melodies for the chorus. I think you just got lazy there when you wrote me. After all, didn't you write me for a class? You had a tight schedule and you kinda rushed me at the end...*

Me: You're darned right. And I think that's what gave you that immediacy, that fire! But I *was* a little sloppy in the chorus.

PR: *So now that we can own up to it, let's get to work.*

Me: Do I have to ?

PR: *If you want me to be as good as I can be...*

Me: Got any hints?

PR: *Yeh, I don't soar in the chorus. I kinda fall on my face. That's okay for some songs, but I'm supposed to be uplifting. GIVE ME SOME UPLIFT! The melody travels down — make it go up instead.*

Me: I see what you mean.

PR: *The chorus should be longer, too, and while you're at it, give it a turnaround. You know, Babs, you cop out a lot in your choruses...and you know that's not cool. Come on, give me a little workout..try out some possibilities.*

Me: Alright, alright, alright...

**Now turn the page for step-by-step
instructions on doing your own dialogue.**

DOING YOUR OWN DIALOGUE:

1.   Think of an incomplete song you've written.

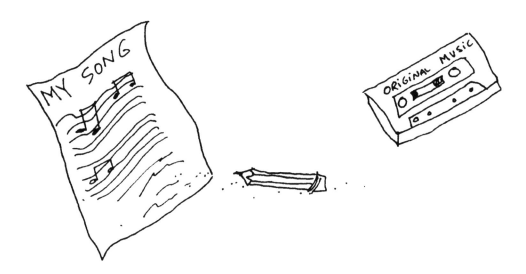

2.   State the reason you want to dialogue with this song.

3.   Begin the conversation and continue until it feels right to stop.

4.   After finishing, read aloud what you've written. If alone, tape record yourself reading aloud and then listen back to it.

One never knows,
do one.

—Thomas "Fats" Waller

Bibliography

The contemporary songwriter quotes were collected from the following sources:

Boyd, Jenny. *Musicians in Tune.* New York: Fireside, 1992.

Braheny, John, Editor. *Songwriters Musepaper*, National Academy of Songwriters, 6255 Sunset Blvd, Ste. 1023, Hollywood, CA 90028.

Zollo, Paul, Editor. *Songtalk Magazine*, National Academy of Songwriters, 6255 Sunset Blvd, Ste. 1023, Hollywood, CA 90028.

Zollo, Paul. *Songwriters on Songwriting.* Cincinnati: Writer's Digest Books, 1991.

Recommended Reading

Braheny, John. *The Craft and Business of Songwriting.* Cincinnati: Writer's Digest Books, 1988.

Coleman, Bob, and Deborah Neville. *The Great American Idea Book.* New York: W. W. Norton & Company, 1993.

Maisel, Eric. *Staying Sane In The Arts: A Guide for Creative and Performing Artists.* New York: Jeremy P. Tarcher, 1992.

Nachmanovitch, Stephen. *Free Play.* Los Angeles: Jeremy P. Tarcher, 1991.

Ristad, Eloise. *A Soprano On Her Head.* Moab, UT: Real People Press, 1982.

Special Thanks

Among those who, by their inspiration and ideas, have made significant contributions to the evolution and development of the Songwriters Playground, four deserve special mention:

Goldberg, Natalie. *Writing Down the Bones: Freeing the Writer Within.* Boston: Shambhala Books, 1989.

_____. *Wild Mind: Living the Writer's Life.* New York: Bantam Books, 1990.

Kline, Peter. *The Everyday Genius.* Arlington: Great Ocean Publishers, 1988.

Progoff, Ira. *At a Journal Workshop.* New York: Dialogue House Library, 1975.

Swados, Elizabeth. *Listening Out Loud.* New York: Harper Collins, 1985.